The Ultimate Smoothie Recipe Book

By: Orlando Scott

Copyright © 2016

Weight Loss Professor

SINGAPORE

© Copyright 2016 by Orlando Scott - All rights reserved.

The contents of this book may not be reproduced, duplicated or transmitted without direct written permission from the author.

Under no circumstances will any legal responsibility or blame be held against the publisher for any reparation, damages, or monetary loss due to the information herein, either directly or indirectly.

Legal Notice:

This book is copyright protected. This is only for personal use. You cannot amend, distribute, sell, use, quote or paraphrase any part or the content within this book without the consent of the author.

Disclaimer Notice:

Please note the information contained within this document is for educational and entertainment purposes only. Every attempt has been made to provide accurate, up to date and reliable complete information. No warranties of any kind are expressed or implied. Readers acknowledge that the author is not engaging in the rendering of legal, financial, medical or professional advice. The content of this book has been derived from various sources. Please consult a licensed professional before attempting any techniques outlined in this book.

By reading this document, the reader agrees that under no circumstances are is the author responsible for any losses, direct or indirect, which are incurred as a result of the use of information contained within this document, including, but not limited to, —errors, omissions, or inaccuracies.

Contents

Introduction 7

Chapter 1 The Health Benefits of Smoothie Ingredients 9

Chapter 2: Lose Weight the Paleo Way 15

    Pear and Parsley 15

    Banana and Coffee 17

    Healthy Red 18

    Peach and Coconut 19

    Banana and Avocado 20

    Cocoa, Coconut, and Macadamia 21

    Bacon and Chocolate 22

    Fall Harvest 23

    Cranberry and Pumpkin 24

    Banana and Chai 25

    Creamy Orange 26

    Strawberries and Cream 27

    Avocado and Chocolate 28

    Winter Warmer 29

    Tropical Delight 30

    No More Hunger Pangs 31

    Pina Colada 32

    Clementine and Strawberry 33

    Lean Mean and Green 34

    The SuperFruit 35

Almond and Mango 36

Banana and Pumpkin 37

Chapter 3: Going Green 38

Ginger, Apple, and Cucumber 38

Ultimate Green 40

Kale, Banana, and Kiwi 41

Kale Green 42

Super Green 43

Kale, Mango, and Peach 44

Tropical Green 45

Green Chocolate and Banana 46

Green Apple and Ginger 47

Tropical Turmeric 48

Tropical Green 49

Tropical Energy 50

Probiotic Winter Bloating 51

Green Pineapple 52

Chocolate Cherry 53

Cucumber, Kale, and Apple 54

Pineapple Paradise 55

Pineapple and Strawberry 56

Green Mojito 57

Groovy Green 58

The Debloater 59

Thin Mint 60

Chapter 4: Let's Get Fruity 61
    Banana and Ginger 61
    Orange Dream 62
    Banana, Blueberry and Green Tea 63
    Berry Breakfast 64
    Banana, Strawberry, and Orange 65
    Passionate Pineapple 66
    Kiwi and Strawberry 67
    Blueberry and Banana 68
    Papaya, Coconut, and Pineapple 69
    Peach and Strawberry 70
    Mango and Apricot 71
    Watermelon 72
    Berry Good 73
    Morning Sunrise 74
    Berry Vanilla 75
    Tutti-Frutti 76
    Strawberry Smooth 77
    Berry Orange 78
    Blueberry Banana Soy 79
    Mango Banana 80

Chapter 5: Clean Living 81
    Berry Breakfast 81
    Super Green 82
    Kale Supreme 83
    Avocado and Spinach 84

Probiotic Belly Soother 85

Apple, Cucumber, and Avocado 86

Morning Glory 87

Banana, Avocado, and Berry 88

Strawberry Fields Forever 89

Berry Dreams 90

Creamy Banana Orange 91

Goji and Strawberry 92

Blueberry and Ginger 93

Minty Apple Berry 94

Berry Spinach 95

All About the Berries 96

Strawberry Chocolate 97

Mango Silk 98

Berry Potion 99

Morning Dessert 100

Chocolate Raspberry 101

Almond, Banana, and Kale 102

Chapter 6: Top Tip for Healthy Smoothies 103

Conclusion 107

Introduction

Smoothies are one of the biggest trends these days and that's because they are healthy, not to mention quick to make and taste delicious. Smoothies serve a number of purposes; as meal replacements, a part of a detox plan, as part of a weight loss plan and just for fun. You don't need to use anything special to make them so don't worry about diving out to buy the best and most expensive blender or smoothie maker you can find. A simple blender or a hand blender will do in most cases.

There are tons of combinations for smoothies and you can get incredibly creative after a while and try your own mixes. Do stick to the recipes first, though, just to get the hang of how the ingredients blend together. Don't be afraid of some of the ingredients either; many people absolutely hate spinach but it is a big part of many smoothies, purely because of its health properties. It doesn't taste that nice on its own but add a banana and you won't even know the spinach is there!

One more tip before I move on to the different types of smoothies in this book – when you make your smoothies, there is a kind of order to how the ingredients go into the blender – this is the difference between whether you get a good smoothie or a mess that you have to scoop out of the blender with a spoon. The most important thin to remember is to add the ingredients with the most juice to your blender first – the juice should be by the blade. If you put thick heavy ingredients in first, the blades on your blender will clog up and the ingredients won't mix properly.

Many of you will already have heard of the Paleo diet, sometimes known as the Caveman diet. The Paleo diet cuts out a high amount of carbohydrate, virtually all dairy, and refined sugar products, concentrating on natural sugars, good fats, and proteins. Paleo smoothies are an excellent way to pep up the Paleo diet, helping you to shed even more pound, simply because you are blending together the perfect combination of Paleo ingredient.

Green smoothies are all the rage, containing high amounts of green super foods, like spinach, kale, apples, etc. all of these contain high amounts of antioxidants, vitamins, and minerals, required by your body for efficient running and weight loss. If you eat nothing else good all day, starting off with a green smoothie mean that your body is getting everything it needs to thrive.

Many smoothies contain fruit, not just because of their health benefits but because they can take away the bitter taste of some of the other ingredients that might be in your smoothie. Add a banana or a mango for a tropical taste and you won't feel like your smoothies are a chore!

Finally, detox or cleansing smoothies can certainly help you to lose weight, especially when you combine them with the right diet. It's no good drinking a healthy cleansing smoothie and then following it up with unhealthy food. The idea of a cleanse is to cleanse the toxins and poisons from your body so don't supplement it with more. These toxins are not just caused by polluted air, refined sugars, bad fats, and gluten cause them for some people. With the smoothie recipes I am going to give you, you can easily do a three or five-day smoothie cleanse without feeling as though you are starving yourself.

So, it's time to step into the healthy and fun world of smoothies. Before we move on to the recipes, we are going to take a look at the health benefits of some of the ingredients of these smoothies.

Chapter 1
The Health Benefits of Smoothie Ingredients

Your smoothies can contain just about anything you want (including bacon!) and, provided you use the right ingredient for the diet plan or eating choices that you are making, you will most definitely reap the healthy benefits of these foods. In this chapter, we are going to take a look at some of the most popular ingredients and what benefits they provide

- **Raspberries** - packed with antioxidants, raspberries can help to increase your oxygen consumption, enzyme activity in your body and the heat production in your fat cells, thus boosting your metabolism and burning off fat much quicker. They have high levels of phytonutrients and powerful anti-inflammatory properties, making them a serious contender in the cancer-fighting stakes

- **Strawberries** – similar in their profile to raspberries but just that little but sweeter. Strawberries are packed with fiber and vitamin C, giving them a bit of an edge over the humble raspberry and they have been shown to help lower levels of bad (LDL) cholesterol

- **Red Peppers** – these contain a high number of carotenoids, like vitamin E, vitamin C, lycopene, beta-carotene and much more besides. The lycopene and fiber make them a good heart-healthy food because they help to lower LDL cholesterol

- **Tomato** – particularly the Roma variety, as they are full of antioxidants and lycopene. Tomatoes are well known as one of the cancer fighters in the food world

- **Red Cabbage** – another powerhouse food, packed with vitamin C and antioxidants that help with boosting the immune system, anti-aging, and helping your skin to glow. Red cabbage also contains glutamine and amino acid that helps to detoxify and stimulate the liver.
- **Guavas** – Loaded up with antioxidants, a guava contains more vitamin C than an orange does. They also contain a high level of lycopene, fiber, and vitamin A.
- **Papaya** – full of digestive enzymes that help the human body to absorb nutrients and use them properly. They also contain vitamin C, vitamin A, potassium and fiber in high levels.
- **Kale** – one of the best super foods in the world, kale contains plenty of the antioxidants our bodies need, as well as having anti-inflammatory properties and benefits as a cancer fighter. Kale also contains omega 3 fatty acids, beneficial to the heart.
- **Lemon Juice** – lemon is a fantastic food, as it helps your liver to flush the toxins out in a natural way, by acting as a diuretic. It is also an antioxidant as well as having anti-inflammatory properties.
- **Ginger** – ginger contains shoga and gingerol, two compounds that can help your digestive tract to ease the symptoms of constipation, gas, bloating and diarrhea.
- **Turmeric** – turmeric is a liver detoxifier and is also one of the most powerful natural anti-inflammatories in the world.
- **Coconut Water Kefir** - a truly super food, packed full of minerals, enzymes, probiotics and vitamins. This

has three major benefits including stopping cravings for sugar, helping with digestion of any food and can help to tone up the abdomen and get rid of the unsightly belly bulge.

- **Chia Seeds** – An incredibly healthy little seed, the chia is packed full of omega fatty acids that help with a healthy brain function, help to lower cholesterol and fight heart disease. This mighty little seed contains protein, amino acids, fiber, minerals vitamins, iron, antioxidants and calcium.
- **Coconut Oil** – perhaps the most important ingredient for those seeking weight loss is coconut oil. The high level of fatty acids converts body fat into energy, boosting metabolism.
- **Flax Seeds** – flax is another tiny little powerhouse that contains high levels of fiber and fatty acids, helping to boost the immune system, protect the heart, improve brain function, promote soft healthy skin, joint function and much more besides but one of the most important jobs it has s to help eliminate the toxins out of your body
- **Goji Berries** – a tasty addition to any smoothie, the goji berry contains antioxidants and amino acids, as well as vitamins and minerals, making it a super healthy food that can help to heal all manner of ills.
- **Spirulina** – not everything that goes into your smoothie will look or taste glamorous and Spirulina is one of these. Spirulina is, in short, pond algae and, although you may balk at the thought of eating it, bear in mind that it is packed with omega fatty acids and protein.

- **Cacao** – particularly powder and nibs and these contain the two things we love the most – lots of antioxidants and the taste of chocolate. The antioxidants help to boost your immune system and, because of their rich dessert-lie flavor, sweet cravings will soon disappear
- **Avocado** – one of the good fats, avocados contain around 20 minerals, vitamins, and plant compounds, as well as being full of heart healthy fat that keeps you feeling fuller for longer
- **Honey and Bee Pollen** – these are both very potent foods, with honey containing antibacterial properties and loads of antioxidants. Honey can be used to fight seasonal allergy, ease coughs, colds and inflamed throats. Bee pollen contains protein, minerals and vitamins and has long been used as a form of treatment for asthma, acne, fatigue, arthritis and indigestion as well as hoping to fight allergies. A word of advice here, though, if you are making smoothies for children, do not add honey because it can cause infant botulism – perfectly safe for adults though
- **Pineapple** – pineapple contains the highest amount of bromelain, more than any other food in the world. Bromelain is another cancer fighter and can also help fight allergies, sinus infections, asthma, joint pain and help with digestion. It also contains manganese that is needed for strengthening bones and connective tissues.
- **Green Tea** - green tea contains a high level of antioxidants, helps fight cancer, keeps the heart healthy, boosts metabolism and aids in digestion.
- **Kiwifruit** – an excellent source of both soluble and insoluble fiber, helping you to feel fuller for longer and

aiding digestion. It has twice the amount of vitamin C than an orange and high levels of potassium, folate, and vitamin E.

- **Spinach** – like kale, this is another of those wonderful super foods that many people simply don't like. However, it has twice the amount of fiber than any other green and is rich in iron, folate vitamin K and vitamin A. It also contains beta carotene, amongst other antioxidants, that help keep the heart healthy fight against cancer and help with eye health.
- **Broccoli** – an excellent source of vitamin A, vitamin C, and vitamin K, as well as calcium and folate. It contains a high number of phytochemicals that help to fight against cancer as well as being high in fiber.

A Word About Fats

Many people shy away from fat believing it to be bad for them. In actual fact, there is a huge difference in fats and the good ones truly are awesome. Just so you know the difference

Good Fats

- Nut oils, in particular, olive palm, flaxseed, avocado, and coconut
- Animal fats, including butter, lard, ghee, tallow, poultry fat, pork fat, etc.

Bad Fats

- Margarine
- Anything with hydrogenated oil or partially hydrogenated oil
- Trans fats – usually found in margarine, spreads that are butter flavored, etc.

- Processed oils like canola, vegetable, corn, and soybean

Always read the labels on anything you buy but, in short, if you want to eat good fat, eat real butter, meat, bacon, unprocessed hams, avocado and use the right oils for cooking. You will note in the recipes that follow that good fats appear in a number of them.

Chapter 2:
Lose Weight the Paleo Way

The Paleo diet is one of the most popular diets for weight loss and making up a few paleo smoothies is an excellent way to gain all the benefits of the diet without bending a rule or two along the way. The paleo smoothie is a good deal healthier than any that you will buy in a supermarket or a smoothie store. This is because your smoothie won't have any dairy in it and will be made of wholesome natural foods, eliminating problems with the digestive system and also containing healthy fats. This chapter contains 22 paleo smoothie recipes so mix and match and enjoy!

Pear and Parsley

Ingredients

- A small bunch of parsley
- ½ of a medium sized avocado
- 1 Nashi pear
- 1 normal pear
- 1 apple – Granny Smith is best
- 2 medium sized plums
- 6 medium sized bananas
- 1 cup of water
- 1 cup of ice

Method

- Remove the stones from the plums
- Skin the avocado and remove the stone
- Peel the bananas

- Remove the stalks from the apple and pears
- Chop all of the fruit up into rough chunks
- Add them to the blender in the order they are in the ingredients list
- Blend until you have a smooth, creamy consistency

Banana and Coffee

Ingredients

- 1 cup of chilled back coffee
- ½ scoop of protein powder, vanilla
- 10 chunks of frozen banana
- 1-2 tbsp. of coconut butter
- 1 tbsp. of almond butter
- ¼ cup of ice

Method

- Add the ingredients to the blender in the order listed
- Blend until smooth

Healthy Red

Ingredients

- 1 cup of red cabbage, chopped
- ½ a red bell pepper
- 1 tomato – roma variety
- 5 medium sized strawberries
- ½ cup of fresh or frozen raspberries
- 1 cup of cold water
- 1 ice cube – optional

Method

- Add ingredients to the blender one at a time
- Blend until smooth

Peach and Coconut

Ingredients

- 1 cup of chilled full fat coconut milk
- 1 cup of ice
- 2 large peaches, peeled and chopped into chunks
- Lemon zest - fresh

Method

- Put the milk, the ice, and the peaches into your blender
- Grate a little lemon zest in
- Blend on high until smooth

Banana and Avocado

Ingredients

- 1 pitted avocado
- 1 Fresh banana
- 1/3 cup of fresh spinach
- ¼ to ½ cup of water

Method

- Put the ingredients into the blender with ¼ cup of water
- Blend for a minute and test the consistency
- Add more water if required and blend until smooth

Cocoa, Coconut, and Macadamia

Ingredients

- 1 cup of ice cubes
- ¾ cup of coconut milk, unsweetened
- 2 tbsp. crushed macadamia nuts, salted variety
- 2 tbsp. sugar alternative
- 1 tbsp. cocoa powder, unsweetened
- ½ tbsp. vanilla extract
- A pinch of salt

Method

- Add all the ingredients to the blender
- Blend until smooth

Topping – optional

- Top off with whipped coconut cream macadamia nuts and toasted coconut

Bacon and Chocolate

Ingredients

- 1 cup of coconut milk
- 1 tbsp. of cocoa powder
- 1 tbsp. of organic honey or maple syrup
- 1 fresh banana
- 4 slices regular bacon or 2 slices of thick bacon, cooked
- 6 ice cubes

Method

- Add all ingredients to the blender
- Blend until smooth and creamy

Fall Harvest

Ingredients

- 1 apple
- 1 orange
- ½ lemon
- 1 inch frozen ginger stem
- 2 cup fresh spinach
- 1 cup of almond milk
- 1 cup of ice cubes

Method

- Grate the ginger
- Peel the lemon
- Core the apple
- Add everything to the blender and blend until smooth

Cranberry and Pumpkin

Ingredients

- 1 cup of non-dairy milk, your preference
- ½ cup puree from fresh pumpkin
- ¼ cup cranberries, fresh or frozen
- ¼ cup raw cashews, soaked if your blender is not a high powered one (if you cannot eat nuts, use ¼ cup plain Greek yoghurt)
- 1 apple, small, cut into chunks
- ½ peeled orange
- 2 tbsp. coconut cream or coconut butter
- ¾ tbsp. cinnamon
- 5-10 drops of stevia, maple syrup, honey or palm sugar – optional

Method

- Put all of the ingredients into your blender
- Blend until smooth
- If your blender is not high powered, soak the cashews for several hours and then drain. Substitute the orange of orange juice and the apple for applesauce

Banana and Chai

Ingredients

- 2 bananas, frozen
- 2 tbsp. coconut milk
- ¼ tsp vanilla
- ¼ tsp cinnamon
- ¼ tsp cloves
- ¼ tsp ginger
- 1 cup of water

Method

- Add the ingredients to your blender
- Blend until a smooth consistency

Creamy Orange

Ingredients

- 4 medium oranges, peeled, seeds and veins removed
- 1 can of coconut milk
- 2 tbsp. of honey
- 1 tbsp. vanilla
- Ice cubes

Method

- Put all of the liquids into your blender and blend until you have a smooth consistency
- Add the ice and blend again

Strawberries and Cream

Ingredients

- 1 cup strawberries, frozen (do not thaw them)
- 1 tbsp. cashews, raw
- 1 avocado, not too ripe, peeled, stone removed and diced
- 1 cup of water or your choice of non-dairy milk
- 1 tbsp. organic honey
- 1 tbsp. hulled hemp hearts or ground flaxseed

Method

- Place all the ingredients in the blender together
- Blend until smooth

Avocado and Chocolate

Ingredients

- 1 ripe avocado
- 2 bananas, frozen
- ½ cup raspberries, frozen or fresh
- 1-2 tbsp. cocoa powder, unsweetened variety
- 2 cups of coconut or almond milk

Method

- Cut the banana and avocado into chunks
- Add to the blender and blend until smooth

Winter Warmer

Ingredients

- 1 apple, core removed and cut into chunks (peel it if your blender is not high powered)
- ½ cup water (substitute with yoghurt for a creamier smoothie)
- ¼ tsp vanilla extract
- 1 tsp organic honey or maple syrup
- ¼ tsp of ground cinnamon
- A pinch of nutmeg and a pinch of allspice
- A scoop of protein powder - optional

Method

- Put the apple, water, honey/syrup, vanilla, and spices into the blender
- Blend until a smooth consistency and then transfer to a mug
- Microwave for 2 minutes on high
- Sprinkle cinnamon over the top and a little whipped coconut cream if you like

Tropical Delight

Ingredients

- ¼ pineapple
- 1 medium apple
- 1 banana
- 1 cup of coconut or almond milk
- 1 tbsp. MCT oil – 100%

Method

- Peel the pineapple and cube the flesh
- Peel, core, and cube the apple
- Slice the banana
- Add the ingredients to the blender and blend on high power until smooth

No More Hunger Pangs

Ingredients

- 1 banana
- ½ an avocado
- 1 cup of fresh spinach (you can also use chard)
- 1 to tbsp. of coconut oil – room temperature
- ¼ cup of coconut milk
- 1 cup of coconut water or ordinary water
- 1 tsp of Ceylon cinnamon (if you use Cassia cinnamon, just ¼ tsp)

Method

- Add all the ingredients to the blender
- Blend until smooth.

Pina Colada

Ingredients

- 1 cup of coconut milk
- 1 packed cup of fresh spinach
- 2 tbsp. of shredded coconut – optional
- ½ banana – frozen
- 1 cup of fresh frozen pineapple chunks

Method

- Put all the ingredient in the blender, starting with the liquids and layering up to the frozen ones
- Blend until smooth

Clementine and Strawberry

Ingredients

- 2 clementine's
- 1 banana, chunked and frozen
- 2 cups of fresh or frozen strawberries

Method

- Let the chunks of banana thaw for 5 minutes and, if using frozen fruit, let it defrost slightly
- Peel the clementine's and remove any seed
- Place all the ingredients into the blender and blend until fully incorporated

Lean Mean and Green

Ingredients

- 2 peeled oranges
- 2 cups of chopped pineapple
- 6 leaves of kale, stems removed
- 2 cups of mango kombucha (juice or water can be substituted)
- 2 cups of water

Method

- Quarter the oranges and put them in the blender first
- Add all the other ingredients and blend on low, increasing your speed
- Blend for 45 seconds on high to finish

The SuperFruit

Ingredients

- 1 cup of ripe papaya chunks
- 3 small guavas
- 1 sprig of fresh parsley
- 1 tsp of fresh lemon juice
- ½ tsp of ginger
- 1 tsp of ginger
- 1 tsp stevia, brown sugar or maple syrup – optional
- 4 ice cubes – optional
- 1 tsp ground flaxseed – optional

Method

- Place all the ingredients into your blender
- Blend on high until smooth

Almond and Mango

Ingredients

- 3 ripe mangoes - preferably Alphonso
- 15 almonds
- ¼ tsp cardamom powder or 3 cardamom
- Sugar as needed
- Ice cubes
- Mint leaves for garnish – optional

Method

- Peel the mangoes and chop them
- Crush the cardamom if using fresh
- Put all ingredient into your blender and blend until smooth

Banana and Pumpkin

Ingredients

- ¾ cup of almond milk, unsweetened
- 1 cup of crushed ice
- ½ banana, frozen
- 1 tsp fine ground flaxseed
- 1/3 cup pureed pumpkin – preferably fresh but canned will do
- 1 – 1 ½ tbsp. maple syrup (grade B)
- ¼ tsp cinnamon
- ¼ tsp nutmeg
- ¼ tsp ginger

Method

- Add all the ingredients to the blender in the order above
- Blend until smooth

Chapter 3: Going Green

If you replace just one of your daily meals with a green smoothie, the health benefits will be tremendous; not only are you getting pretty much everything your body need in one hit, green smoothies can also help you to drop a few pounds. Greens contain a higher level of nutrients than any of the other food groups, as well as a ton of amino acids. You will experience a higher energy level much nicer skin and stronger nails and hair. The one good thing about green smoothies is that the fiber content of the ingredients is retained whereas in juicing, it is all removed and, with a good boost of fiber on a regular basis, your body will soon be ridding itself of toxins. These recipes are packed with fiber as well as other essential vitamins and minerals.

Ginger, Apple, and Cucumber

Ingredients

- 1 cucumber
- 1 good handful of spinach
- 1 apple, seeds removed
- 1 tbsp. fresh ginger, minced
- Juice from one lime
- 1 tbsp. organic honey, maple or agave syrup
- 1 cup of water
- Raw bee pollen – optional

Method

- Take around 60% of the peel from the cucumber
- Put all ingredients in the blender (not the bee pollen) and blend on high until the desired consistency is reached
- Taste, add more honey if needed and blend again
- Sprinkle with bee pollen before serving

Ultimate Green

Ingredients

- 3 cups of organic greens – spinach, collard, kale, etc. – mixed
- 3 cucumbers – Persian
- 1 cup of stemmed parsley
- 1 ½ cups of milk – coconut, hemp, almond, rice, soy
- 1 cup of water
- 2 apples, cored
- ½ lemon, deseeded
- 4 ice cubes

Method

- Place all the ingredients in the blender, liquids first
- Blend on high until smooth
- Add more water if needed

Kale, Banana, and Kiwi

Ingredients

- 2 overripe bananas
- 2 kiwifruits, peeled and cut in half
- 1 tightly packed cup of kale
- 1 cup of milk
- 2 or 3 tbsp. honey
- ½ cup of shaved or crushed ice

Method

- Place all ingredients into the blender
- Blend on high until smooth

Kale Green

Ingredients

- 1 cup of fresh kale
- I cup of pineapple cubes
- 1 banana
- ½ cup of almond milk
- 1 tbsp. freshly squeezed lemon juice
- Ice – optional

Method

- Put all the ingredients in your blender
- Blend until the kale has been fully incorporated

Super Green

Ingredients

- ¾ cup chunks of pineapple
- 1 frozen banana, peeled and chunked
- 1 tsp fresh orange zest – optional
- 1 tsp ground flaxseed
- 1 cup of baby fresh kale
- 1 cup of soy milk, almond milk, coconut water or non-fat milk

Method

- Combine everything together in your blender
- Blend until incorporated and smooth
- Chill or serve over ice

Kale, Mango, and Peach

Ingredients

- ½ a banana
- 1 whole pear, deseeded and sliced
- 1 p of low-fat Greek yoghurt
- ¾ cup of water
- 1 ½ cups peaches, frozen
- 1 cup mango, frozen
- 1 ½ tsp honey

Method

- Put the pear, banana, yoghurt, water and kale in the blender and blend until fully incorporated
- Add the rest of the ingredients and blend to a smooth puree
- Add more water if needed

Tropical Green

Ingredients

- ½ cup of cold water
- ¼ cup of Greek yoghurt, non-fat variety
- 1 packed cup of fresh spinach
- 1 cup of mango chunks, frozen
- 1 cup of pineapple chunks, frozen
- 1 banana, frozen

Method

- Place everything in the blender in the order listed
- Blend on medium high for about 40 seconds

Green Chocolate and Banana

Ingredients

- ½ a ripe banana
- ½ a small apple
- 1 generous handful of fresh spinach
- 1 heaped tbsp. of almond butter
- 1 tbsp. cacao powder, organic
- ½ cup of almond milk
- Ice cubes

Method

- Add all the ingredients to your blender
- Blend until smooth

Green Apple and Ginger

Ingredients

- 1 apple, cored and quartered
- ½ cup fresh spinach
- 1-inch piece of ginger, peeled
- 1 tbsp. golden flaxseed
- 1/3 cup Greek yoghurt
- 1 cup of milk – your choice
- Ice

Method

- Put everything into your blender
- Blend until smooth

Tropical Turmeric

Ingredients

- 2 cups of fresh kale
- 2 cups of coconut milk
- 2 cups of pineapple
- 1 cup of mango
- Juice from ½ a lemon
- 1 tbsp. fresh ginger root
- ¼ - ½ tsp ground turmeric

Method

- Blend the coconut milk and kale together first until smooth
- Add the rest of the ingredients, blend until fully incorporated

Tropical Green

Ingredients

- 1 large banana, ripe and frozen
- ½ cup of mango chunks, frozen
- 1 large handful of mixed greens
- ½ cup of pineapple, fresh or frozen
- 1 ½ cups coconut milk, cold
- Juice and zest of one fresh lime

Method

- Put all of the ingredients into your blender
- Pulse until incorporated and smooth

Tropical Energy

Ingredients

- ¾ cup of almond milk
- 2 medium bananas, sliced and frozen
- 2 cup of pineapple chunks, fresh
- 2 generous cups of fresh kale

Method

- Add all of the ingredients to your blender in the recipe order
- Blend for at least 3 minutes on high power
- Scrape the sides as needed and add more milk if it is too thick

Probiotic Winter Bloating

Ingredients

- 2 cups of coconut water kefir
- 1 roughly chopped apple
- 1 roughly chopped pear
- 1 peeled and chopped cucumber
- 2 cups fresh spinach
- ½ ripe avocado
- 2 stalks of celery
- 1 tbsp. fresh ginger, chopped roughly
- Juice from a fresh lemon
- Juice from a fresh lime

Method

- Add the ingredients to the blender in the recipe order
- Blend on high until smooth

Green Pineapple

Ingredients

- ½ cup of almond milk, unsweetened
- 1/3 cup plain Greek yoghurt, non-fat variety
- 1 cup of fresh baby spinach
- 1 cup of banana slices, frozen
- ½ cup of pineapple chunks, frozen
- 1 tbsp. chia seed
- ½ tsp organic honey or maple syrup – optional

Method

- Blend the milk and yoghurt together first
- Add the rest of the ingredient and blend together until smooth

Chocolate Cherry

Ingredients

- 2 ½ cups of vanilla almond milk, unsweetened
- 3 cups of fresh baby spinach
- 2 cups of sweet cherries, pitted, fresh or frozen
- 1 banana
- 2 tbsp. cocoa powder, unsweetened
- 1 tbsp. of agave nectar

Method

- Blend the milk and the spinach together until the spinach is pureed
- Add the rest of the ingredients and blend together for a couple of minutes

Cucumber, Kale, and Apple

Ingredients

- ½ cup of water
- 2 ½ cups of green grapes
- 1 orange, peeled, deseeded and cut in half
- ½ lemon, peeled and deseeded
- ½ a cucumber, peeled and chunked
- ½ apple, deseeded – green, not red
- 1 cup of kale with the ribs removed
- 1 cup of romaine lettuce
- 1 cup of fresh parsley, flat leaf
- 1 cup of mango or pineapple chunks, frozen
- 2 cups of ice
- 2 tbsp. of an antioxidant smoothie mix

Method

- Place the ingredients in the blender in recipe order
- Blend until smooth

Pineapple Paradise

Ingredients

- ¾ cup of water
- 2 cups of pineapple chunks, fresh or thawed
- 1 ripe avocado, pitted and halved
- 2 cups of fresh spinach
- ½ cup of ice cubes

Method

- Add to the blender in the order of the recipe
- Blend until smooth

Pineapple and Strawberry

Ingredients

- 1 ½ cups of fresh or frozen strawberries
- 1 cup of fresh pineapple chunks
- 2 cups of fresh spinach
- 1 cup of water

Method

- Add the water to your blender first and then add the soft fruit
- The spinach goes in last, blend on high power for 30 seconds or until smooth

Green Mojito

Ingredients

- ½ cup of soy milk
- 1 banana, frozen
- 1 cup of fresh baby spinach
- 1 tsp vanilla extract
- Juice from ½ a fresh lime
- ½ cup of spearmint, fresh
- Ice cubes

Method

- Place all the ingredients except the ice and spearmint in the blender and pulse until combined
- Add the ice and spearmint and blend together until smooth

Groovy Green

Ingredients

- ½ a pear
- 1 cucumber, seeded and chopped
- ¼ cup fresh dill, chopped
- 1 small avocado
- 1 cup of fresh baby spinach
- 2 tbsp. fresh lime juice
- 1-inch fresh peeled ginger root
- 1 cup of pineapple, frozen
- 1 ¼ cups of water
- 3 or 4 ice cubes
- 1 tbsp. chia seed – optional

Method

- Put everything except the ice and chia into the blender
- Blend until smooth
- Add the ice, pulse until mixed in
- Stir the chia seeds in

The Debloater

Ingredients

- ½ cup of pineapple
- ½ cup of papaya
- 1 banana, frozen
- ¼ of a cucumber
- 1 cup of coconut water, chilled
- 2 cups of fresh spinach
- 4 ice cubes

Method

- Put all the ingredient into your blender, liquid first
- Blend until smooth

Thin Mint

Ingredients

- ¾ cup of Greek yoghurt, non-fat variety
- ¼ cup of packed fresh mint
- 1 cup of almond milk
- ¼ cup of dark chocolate chips
- 1 cup of baby spinach
- 1 tbsp. maple syrup
- 2 cups of ice

Method

- Put all ingredients into the blender
- Blitz until smooth

Chapter 4:
Let's Get Fruity

So many people avoid fruit because of its sugar content but it is important to remember that the sugar in fruit is natural. Obviously, if you are trying to lose weight, you shouldn't eat too much fruit because even natural fructose can pile on the pounds if you over do it. That said, fruits of all kinds contain numerous health benefits. They are packed with minerals and vitamins, not to mention other compounds that we need and the humble berry is the healthiest of the lot, loaded with antioxidants that help to rid our bodies of unwanted toxins.

Banana and Ginger

Ingredients

- 1 sliced banana
- ¾ cup of vanilla yoghurt
- 1 tbsp. organic honey
- ½ tsp fresh ginger, grated

Method

- Place everything into your blender
- Blitz until completely smooth

Orange Dream

Ingredients

- 1 peeled orange
- ¼ cup of yoghurt, fat-free
- 2 tbsp. orange juice concentrate, frozen
- ¼ tsp of vanilla extract
- 4 ice cubes

Method

- Add all the ingredients to the blender
- Pulse until smooth

Banana, Blueberry and Green Tea

Ingredients

- 3 tbsp. of water
- 2 tsp honey
- 1 green tea bag
- 1 ½ cups of blueberries frozen
- 1 medium banana
- ¾ cup vanilla soy milk, light

Method

- Microwave the water until steaming hot
- Add the tea bag and leave it to brew for three minutes
- Take the bag out ad add the honey, stirring until it is completely dissolved
- Put the berries, milk and banana into the blender and pulse until combined
- Add the tea and blend on high until smooth

Berry Breakfast

Ingredients

- 1 cup of raspberries, frozen
- ¾ cup rice or almond milk, unsweetened and chilled
- ¼ cup cherries, pitted and frozen
- 1 ½ tbsp. honey
- 2 tsp fresh ginger, finely grated
- 1 tsp ground flaxseed
- 2 tsp fresh lemon juice

Method

- Add all ingredients to the blender
- Puree until combined and smooth

Banana, Strawberry, and Orange

Ingredients

- 1 cup of plain yoghurt, non-fat
- 1 banana
- ½ cup of unsweetened orange juice
- 6 strawberries, frozen

Method

- Add all ingredients to the blender
- Blend for 20 seconds, scrape the sides and blend for 15 more seconds

Passionate Pineapple

Ingredients

- 1 cup of vanilla yoghurt, low fat
- 1 cup of pineapple chunks
- 6 ice cubes

Method

- Put the ice and yoghurt in the blender and pulse until combined
- Add the pineapple and whip until smooth

Kiwi and Strawberry

Ingredients

- 1 ¼ cup of apple juice, chilled
- 1 sliced banana
- 1 sliced kiwifruit
- 5 strawberries, frozen
- 1 ½ tsp organic honey

Method

- Combine all ingredients in the blender
- Blend until smooth

Blueberry and Banana

Ingredients

- 1 ¼ cups of soy milk, light
- ½ sliced frozen banana
- ½ cup of frozen blueberries
- 2 tsp sugar or sugar alternative
- 1 tsp vanilla extract

Method

- Put 1 cup of milk into the blender
- Add the rest of the ingredients except the milk and blend on high
- Add the rest of the milk if you need it

Papaya, Coconut, and Pineapple

Ingredients

- 1 papaya, chunked
- 1 cup of plain yoghurt, fat-free
- ½ cup of fresh pineapple, chunked
- ½ cup ice, crushed
- 1 tsp coconut extract
- 1 tsp ground flaxseed

Method

- Add the ingredients to the blender in the recipe order
- Blend on high for about 30 seconds

Peach and Strawberry

Ingredients

- 1 cup of milk, 1%
- 2 tbsp. vanilla yoghurt, low-fat
- ½ cup of peaches, frozen
- ½ cup of strawberries
- 1/8 tsp of ginger powder
- 2 tsp whey protein powder
- 3 ice cubes

Method

- Add the liquid ingredients with the whey and blend until combined
- Add the rest of the ingredients and blend on high until smooth

Mango and Apricot

Ingredients

- 6 apricots, peeled and chopped
- 2 mangoes, peeled and chopped
- 1 cup of low-fat milk or plain yoghurt
- 4 tsp lemon juice
- ¼ tsp vanilla extract
- 8 ice cubes

Method

- Put everything except the ice into the blender and blend for 8 seconds
- Add ice and blitz for a further 6 to 8 seconds

Watermelon

Ingredients

- 2 cups of watermelon, chopped
- ¼ cup of no-fat milk
- 2 cups of ice

Method

- Blend the milk and the watermelon together for 15 seconds
- Add the ice and blend for a further 20 seconds

Berry Good

Ingredients

- 1 ½ cups of strawberries chopped
- 1 cup of fresh blueberries
- ½ cup of fresh raspberries
- 2 tbsp. honey
- 1 tsp fresh lemon juice
- ½ cup of ice cubes

Method

- Add all the ingredients to the blender
- Blitz until smooth

Morning Sunrise

Ingredients

- 1 banana
- 1 cup of chilled apricot nectar
- 1 cup of low-fat yoghurt, peach flavor
- 1 tbsp. lemonade concentrate, frozen
- ½ cup of chilled club soda

Method

- Add everything except for the soda to the blender and blend for 30 seconds
- Stir the soda in and serve

Berry Vanilla

Ingredients

- ½ cup of raspberries, frozen
- ½ cup of strawberries, frozen
- ¾ cup pineapple juice, unsweetened
- 1 cup vanilla yoghurt, fat-free

Method

- Blend the fruit and juice together
- Add the yogurt and blend again until smooth

Tutti-Frutti

Ingredients

- ½ cup of strawberries or other berries, frozen
- ½ cup of crushed pineapple in juice
- ½ cup plain yoghurt
- ½ cup of ripe banana, sliced
- ½ cup orange juice

Method

- Add all the ingredients to the blender
- Blend until smooth

Strawberry Smooth

Ingredients

- 1 cup of skimmed milk
- 1 cup of strawberries, frozen
- 1 tbsp. flaxseed oil
- 1 tbsp. pumpkin or sunflower seeds

Method

- Blend the strawberries and milk for 1 minute
- Add the oil and seeds and stir in

Berry Orange

Ingredients

- 1 cup of frozen berries
- ½ cup of low-fat yogurt
- ½ cup of orange juice

Method

- Put all ingredients in the blender and pulse for 30 seconds
- Blend for a further 30 seconds until smooth

Blueberry Banana Soy

Ingredients

- 1 cup of vanilla soy milk
- ½ cup of blueberries, frozen
- ½ cup of cornflakes
- 1 sliced banana, frozen

Method

- Add all the ingredients to the blender and blend for 20 seconds
- Scrape the sides and blend for a further 15 seconds

Mango Banana

Ingredients

- 1 cup of pineapple chunks in juice
- 1 cup of frozen vanilla yoghurt fat-free
- 1 ripe chopped and peeled mango
- 1 sliced banana
- Crushed ice

Method

- Blend all the ingredients except the ice until smooth
- Add the ice gradually to the mixture and blend until pureed.

Chapter 5: Clean Living

When you feel washed out, worn down and fed up with life, a detox smoothie is just the thing to pick you up. In order to give your body a break and detox it, you must give it the food it needs to clean itself out, food that is packed full of minerals and vitamins to help it function. Add one of these smoothies to your daily routine and you will feel better than you ever have done.

Berry Breakfast

Ingredients

- 1 cup of raspberries, frozen
- ¾ cup of almond or rice milk, chilled and unsweetened
- ¼ cup of cherries, pitted and frozen
- 1 ½ tbsp. organic honey
- 2 tsp ginger, freshly grated
- 1 tsp ground flaxseed
- 2 tsp fresh squeezed lemon juice

Method

- Put all the ingredients in the blender
- Blend on high until smooth

Super Green

Ingredients

- 1 ¼ cups chopped kale with the ribs and stems removed
- 1 ¼ cups of mango, cubed and frozen
- 2 stalks of celery, chopped
- 1 cup of orange or tangerine juice, chilled
- ¼ cup chopped parsley, flat leaf
- ¼ cup fresh mint chopped

Method

- Place all ingredients into the blender
- Blend on high until smooth

Kale Supreme

Ingredients

- ½ a pear
- ½ an avocado
- ½ a cucumber
- ½ a lemon
- A good handful of cilantro
- 1 packed cup of kale
- ½ inch of ginger root
- ½ cup of coconut water
- 1 scoop of protein powder
- 1 cup soy milk

Method

- Put all the ingredients in the blender
- Blend until smooth

Avocado and Spinach

Ingredients

- ½ a pear
- ½ an avocado
- 1 cup of tightly packed spinach
- ½ cup of coconut milk
- 1 cup of almond milk
- 1 scoop of protein powder
- 1 tsp chia seeds

Method

- Add all the ingredients to your blender
- Blend until completely smooth

Probiotic Belly Soother

Ingredients

- 1 cup of fresh papaya
- 1 cup of coconut kefir – cultured coconut milk or coconut yoghurt are good substitutes
- Juice from a ½ a fresh lime
- 1 tbsp. fresh honey

Method

- Add all the ingredients to your blender in the recipe order
- Blend until smooth

Apple, Cucumber, and Avocado

Ingredients

- 5 large lettuce leaves – Romaine is best
- ½ a Granny Smith apple
- ¼ an avocado
- ½ a cucumber
- ½ cup of jicama
- Generous handful of cilantro
- 1 large lime
- 4 scoops of protein powder – hemp is the best
- 1 Medjool date
- ½ cup coconut or soy milk

Method

- Add all the ingredients in the recipe order
- Blend on high until smooth

Morning Glory

Ingredients

- 1 cucumber
- Generous handful of fresh kale
- Generous handful of romaine lettuce
- 3 celery stalks
- 1 large stem of broccoli
- 1 large green apple, cut into quarters
- ½ lemon, peeled and quartered
- ½ cup soy milk

Method

- Prepare the fruit and vegetables by washing and chopping
- Add everything to the blender and blend until smooth

Banana, Avocado, and Berry

Ingredients

- 1 avocado
- 1 cup of blueberries
- 1 banana
- 1 generous handful of kale, spinach or romaine
- ½ cup coconut milk
- Stevia to taste – optional

Method

- Place the ingredients in the blender in the order of the recipe
- Blend on high power until smooth and fully combined

Strawberry Fields Forever

Ingredients

- 3 cups of cashew milk or your preference of non-dairy milk
- 2 cups of strawberries, fresh not frozen
- 1 tbsp. of fresh lemon zest
- 1 small orange, peeled and seeded
- 1 banana
- 1 ½ cups of spinach, loosely packed

Method

- Place all ingredients into your blender
- Blend on high power for a few minutes until everything is thoroughly combined

Berry Dreams

Ingredients

- 1 cup of coconut, hemp or rice milk
- 1 cup of blackberries, frozen
- ½ cup of fresh or frozen strawberries
- 1 generous handful of fresh kale
- ½ an avocado
- ½ tsp of fresh lime juice
- ½ tsp vanilla
- 1 or 2 tbsp. of ground flax seed, ground chia seed or a mixture of both
- Ice cubes – optional

Method

- Add the ingredients in the order of the recipe
- Blend until completely combined and smooth

Creamy Banana Orange

Ingredients

- 1 cup of coconut rice or hemp milk
- ½ a bunch of fresh kale
- 1 banana
- ½ an orange
- 1 tsp of vanilla
- 1 tsp of cinnamon
- 1 dash of cayenne pepper
- 1 or 2 tbsp. ground flax and/or chia seed
- ½ cup of crushed ice

Method

- Put everything in the blender
- Blend until completely smooth

Goji and Strawberry

Ingredients

- 1 cup of coconut kefir water
- ½ cup of coconut milk
- 1 banana, frozen
- ¼ cup of strawberries, frozen
- 3 tbsp. Goji berries

Method

- Place the ingredients, in order, in the blender
- Blitz until you have a smooth puree

Blueberry and Ginger

Ingredients

- 1 cup of almond milk, or any other milk of your choice
- ¼ cup of blueberries
- 1 frozen banana
- 3 tbsp. ginger juice
- Ice - optional

Method

- Blend everything together until a smooth consistency is reached
- Add ice if required and pulse until it has broken up

Minty Apple Berry

Ingredients

- ½ an apple, green not red
- 2 tbsp. hemp hearts
- 8 leaves of fresh mint
- 3 or 4 leaves of any green leaf lettuce
- ¼ cup of berry blend, fresh or frozen
- 1 cup of coconut or almond soy milk

Method

- Add everything to the blender
- Blend on high until the desired consistency is reached

Berry Spinach

Ingredients

- 1 ½ cups of milk, dairy free
- ½ large peeled cucumber, sliced
- 1 cup of blueberries
- ½ packed cup of spinach
- 1 tbsp. ground flax seed
- 1 tbsp. chia seed
- Stevia or other sugar substitute to taste
- Ice – optional

Method

- Add all ingredients to the blender and blitz for one minute
- Taste, add sugar substitute and blend for 15 seconds
- Add ice if wanted and blend until incorporated

All About the Berries

Ingredients

- 1 ½ cups of mixed berries – blackberries blueberries and raspberries
- ½ cup of coconut milk
- 1 cup of filtered water
- 1/8 cup of rolled oats

Method

- Add everything to the blender
- Blend on high for as long as it takes to reach a smooth consistency

Strawberry Chocolate

Ingredients

- 1 tbsp. cocoa powder, dark
- ½ cup coconut milk
- ½ cup strawberries, fresh or frozen
- 1 cup of ice

Method

- Add everything to the blender
- Blend until you have a smooth, frothy consistency

Mango Silk

Ingredients

- ¼ cup of fresh or frozen mango cubes
- ¼ cup of avocado
- ½ cup fresh mango juice
- 1 tbsp. fresh lime juice

Method

- Blend everything together until smooth
- Serve chilled or over ice

Berry Potion

Ingredients

- 1 cup of coconut milk
- 1 cup of fresh or frozen blueberries
- 1 cup of fresh or frozen blueberries
- ½ cup for fresh or frozen raspberries
- ½ cup of fresh or frozen blackberries
- 2 tbsp. soaked Goji berries
- 1 tbsp. coconut oil
- 1 tbsp. ground flaxseed
- 2 pitted dates

Method

- Add all ingredients to the blender, liquid first
- Blend until smooth

Morning Dessert

Ingredients

- ½ cup of almond milk
- 1 whole banana
- 2 tbsp. of organic hazelnut butter
- 1 tsp of cocoa powder
- 1 tbsp. of organic maple syrup or honey

Method

- Blend everything together until smooth
- Serve over ice or chilled

Chocolate Raspberry

Ingredients

- ½ cup of almond milk
- ¼ cup of dark chocolate chips
- 1 cup of raspberries, fresh or frozen

Method

- Blend together until fully combined
- Serve with ice or chilled first

Almond, Banana, and Kale

Ingredients

- ½ cup of almond milk
- 2 tbsp. of organic almond butter
- 1 generous handful of kale
- 1 banana

Method

- Blend until completely smooth
- Serve with crushed ice or chilled

Chapter 6:
Top Tip for Healthy Smoothies

Everyone who makes smoothies will tell you their own tips for how to make the best ones. There are a few tricks to smoothie success and I have 20 of them for you here. Whether you want an idea for new ingredients a better way to make sure you get enough nutrition or are looking to lose weight, clear your skin and boost your energy, the smoothie is the right choice for you and are a great deal more fun that water or fruit.

Change the Ingredients

You don't have to stick to the tried and tested – change your fruits and vegetables to suit you and to get different health benefits. Use what is in season at the time you make your smoothies. If you make green smoothies don't stick to the same greens every time, rotate them regularly to stop yourself from getting bored

Fresh is Best

The fresher your ingredient are, the better the flavor will be and the more nutrients will be in your smoothie. Use organic as much as you can – this doesn't just cut out the pesticides and increase the nutrients, it also makes the smoothie taste much better

Use Healthy Tea

Instead of water or juice, even milk, substitute a healthy tea as a boost to the nutritional stakes. You can make it in advance and store it for use when you need it. If you are trying to solve a particular issue with your health, there is no doubt that there is an herb or two that will help and can be made into a lovely tea.

Keep it Sweet

But not with regular refined sugar. Use dates as a way of adding a sweet taste – soak them thoroughly first and remove pits. If you must use a sweetener, avoid those with aspartame n them. Use maple syrup, agave, honey and stevia instead Winter fruit might not have the sweetness that you want so substitute water in a recipe for fruit juice

Get Juicing

You can juice up your fruits and vegetables as a base for a smoothie but do be aware that you may be losing out on fiber and nutrients that way

Use that Kefir

Coconut kefir is full of probiotics that pack a healthy punch, improve your digestive system and help your body to use the nutrients properly

Spice Things Up

Spices can add both nutrition and flavor to a smoothie so don't be afraid to play about with them. Some are quite strong so don't overdo it but certainly nutmeg, ginger, cayenne and cinnamon are good ones to add.

Protein Power

Protein powders can provide a good boost, especially if you are looking to add bulk to your muscle. Do use a good quality one though as cheap ones are full of nasty "surprises".

Add Those Good Fats

Avocado, hemp oil, flax oils and coconut oils, or cream will add a good dose of healthy fat to your smoothie, helping you to feel fuller for longer and give you more energy.

Salt is Good

Use a high-quality salt, like the Himalayan pink, Celtic sea salt or Redmond salt in your smoothies, where needed. Don't overdo it and don't use cheap salt because they lack the minerals n the good quality ones.

Superfoods!

Try a lot of different ones and see which ones you like, which one make you feel good. There are lots to choose from and each one provides plenty of nutrient and lots of health benefit.

Add Those Seeds

Chia, hemp, and flaxseed are excellent sources of nutrition and fiber ad will enhance any smoothie.

Herby Goodness

Use Chinese herb powders to boost your smoothies, like ginseng, rhodiola, and astragalus.

Don't Skimp Your Base

Always use filtered water, or high-quality juices and milk as your smoothie bases. Cheap and cheerful and cheap and nasty and definitely avoid the own brands.

Green Power

Use superfood powders to give your smoothie a boost of green nutrients in an instant

Spice up your Ice Cubes

You don't have to use plain water in your ice. Use coconut water to add extra potassium, magnesium, and other electrolytes.

Use the Mushroom

Mushroom powders are excellent for boosting the immune system and can be added to just about any smoothie you want.

Banana Cubes

Bananas, as you may have noticed, is one of the staples of many smoothies. If you use frozen ones a lot, have a go at this. Peel your ripe bananas and break them up into mall chunks. Put the chunks in a big Ziploc bag and freeze them. You can do this with several bananas at once and then just pick out as much or as little as you need at a time

Make Your Smoothies Kid-Friendly

We all know that kids can be fussy eaters and more often than not it will be the color or the smoothie texture that puts them off. Start simple and gradually add in ingredients like spinach over time, let them get used to it until they are downing them like pros!

Have a lot of Fun

Smoothies are fun and you should get everyone in the family involved. Make your own smoothies with ingredient choices from everyone – you never know what you might turn up with!

Conclusion

I hope you enjoyed trying out these delicious smoothie recipes and I hope you had some fun with them as well. Smoothies are an excellent way to make sure that you get all of the vitamins and minerals that you need on a daily basis and are also good for weight loss. One word of warning here – even though these smoothies may be, do not be tempted to use them as a meal replacement for every meal unless you are on a set detox plan, i.e. 3 or 5 days.

You do need to eat other foods as well, particularly proteins and good carbohydrates and, although the smoothies are incredibly healthy, they are not designed for long-term meal replacement use. Obviously, you can replace one meal each day on a permanent basis and you can have smoothies as treats or as a dessert, especially when you think you might give in and have something you shouldn't.

Please be sensible and, if you are following a diet plan, please make sure your smoothies fit in with that pan otherwise it will all be to waste. The recipes in this book cover just about every diet plan you could possibly be on and there really is something for everyone – even bacon!

Finally, if you enjoyed this book, then I'd like to ask you for a favor, would you be kind enough to leave a review for this book on Amazon? It'd be greatly appreciated!

Thank you and good luck

Made in the USA
Middletown, DE
30 October 2016